3714

4

Antonin Dvorak
Quintet in A Major, Opus 81

1

Printed in Canada

music minus one cello

MMO

Antonin
Dvorak

Quintet in A minor, Opus 81
for Piano, Two Violins, Viola and Cello

MMO CD 3714

Photo: Philip Jensen-Carter

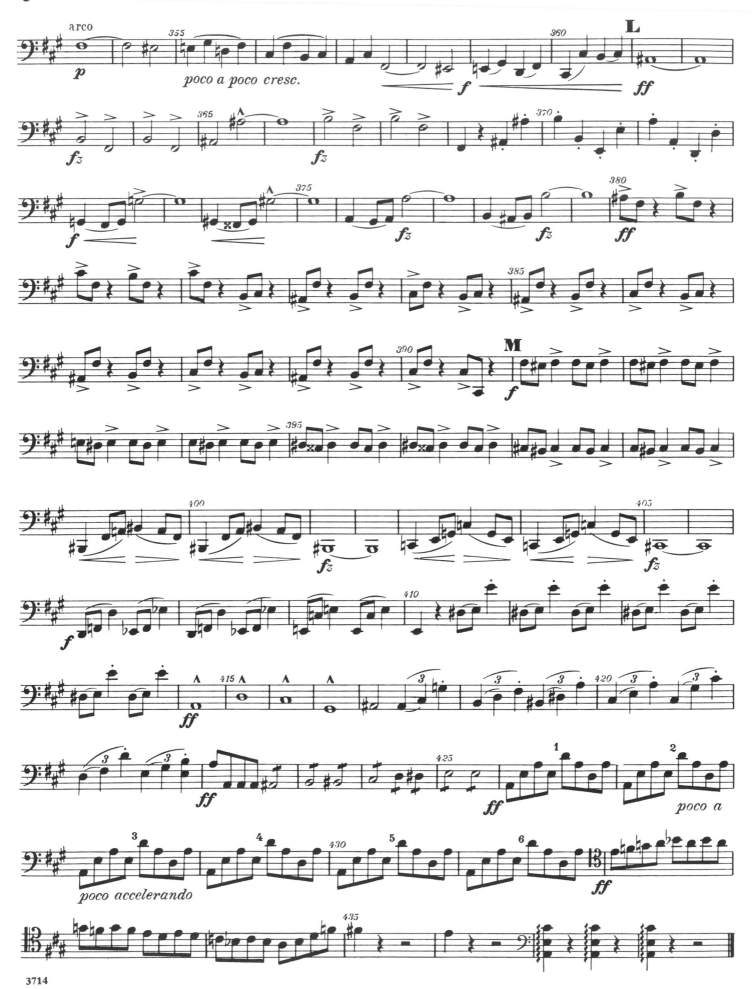

2
DUMKA

Vivace (quasi l'istesso tempo)

poco a poco string.

poco ritenuto al - - - Tempo 1

3

SCHERZO Furiant

11

3714

4

Finale

MMO CD 3714

Music Minus One

DVORAK
Quintet in A Major, Opus 81
Cello

Dvorak Piano Quintet in A Major

This quintet, regarded as one of the finest of its genre, was written during a time of constructive self-examination. It was in 1887, after an unsatisfactory attempt to revise an earlier piano quintet also in A (Op. 5), that Dvorak, happy in the peaceful beauty of his new summer estate, Vysoka, realized his ideas to compose a delightfully fresh and buoyant work.

The style of the Czech master is epitomized here by the use of a full spectrum of emotions, the Slavonic melodies and all-pervasive rhythms, and the wide range of instrumental coloring.

The first movement establishes the overall mood pattern of the work. It passes from pensive brooding through exuberance to tranquility. The second movement is a *"dumka"* in rondo form with the elegiac subject recurring between happier and more propulsive sections. The scherzo that follows is entitled *"furiant."* Although it does not use the characteristics alternating of duple and triple rhythm of the dance, it has wonderful melodic contrasts. A lively *"allegro"* ensues with bright rhythms, counterpoints and a Slavonic theme, all fully developed to form a masterful conclusion.

— Beverley Gertsman

Recorded at Lincoln Sound Center, N.Y.C.
Robert Kard – Producer
Andrew L. Miller – Recording Engineer
© Copyright 1974

Music Minus One 50 Executive Boulevard Elmsford, New York 10523 - 1325

Fax 914 - 592 3575   E mail mmomus@aol.com   Phone 914 592 1188